T0322143

EMBRACE YOUR VILLAIN ERA

by Sarah Thompson

POP PRESS

Contents

The Wisdom of Wednesday Addams

o you ever feel like you're always putting other people first? Do you find yourself sidelining your own needs just so you can keep everyone else happy? Or maybe you're afraid to stand up for yourself, or simply to say no to things, because you're worried about being the villain in someone else's story?

If any of this sounds familiar, then you could probably do with Wednesday's wisdom. In case you've never come across her before, Wednesday Addams is a fearless feminist icon who knows herself and never compromises her authenticity, for anyone. An original rebel who'll always fight for her cause, Wednesday's unique approach to life can teach us all a few things when it comes to standing in your power and being unapologetically you — even if it means making other people uncomfortable sometimes.

This wise and witty icon, with her trademark plaits and big shirt collars, has a super-kooky family and some fairly unusual hobbies and interests. But Wednesday never feels ashamed of who she is or where she's come from. Instead of shrinking herself to fit other people's ideas of what and who she should be, she wears her individuality with pride. And if people don't like her for it, she doesn't worry about trying to please them. Wednesday knows that what other people think of her is really not her concern, and if that means being the bad guy in other people's narratives, then so be it.

But Wednesday isn't mean to others. Sure, she can be forthright at times, and she certainly has some interesting ways of dealing with anyone who crosses her . . . Some people can find that hard to deal with, especially if they're not used to meeting a young woman with such uncompromising self-belief. But to the people she cares about, Wednesday is a loyal and faithful friend, an authentic and interesting human being with a richly layered personality and a ton of useful skills. Who wouldn't want to be friends with someone like that? And if they don't? Well, you know what Wednesday would say about that . . .

This book is divided into eight sections, each tackling the big themes in life, designed to help you step into your power. You can read it all in one go, or make like Wednesday and dip into it when you need a little quiet time away from the noise and hubbub of daily life. Making positive changes and letting go of unhelpful relationships can be scary at times, but rest assured that you will find all the comfort as well as the confidence boost you need to keep going in these pages.

In *Family*, you'll find advice on coping with your relatives, learn how your ancestry can inspire you when you are exploring your own identity and that there isn't a 'one-size-fits-all' solution when it comes to the family unit. In *Friends*, be inspired by Wednesday's fiercely loyal friendship style and learn to set boundaries with her zero-tolerance approach to people who don't share her energy. *Home* highlights the importance of making your own space and shows you how to dial up your personality, even in the smallest locations. In *Style*, learn to express yourself with what you wear and how finding your own look and palette can set you free from worry about appearance. *Work* is all about standing in your power in a professional setting, believing in yourself and finding your focus to see your big ideas through. In *Music* and *Creativity*, we'll see how important having a creative practice is and why you should make time for the things you love, too, no matter how weird they are. And in *Love*, learn how Wednesday sets healthy boundaries when it comes to relationships, and why establishing your love language is the first step to an equal, empowering relationship.

So grab a brew (or a quad, black), find a quiet space where you won't be disturbed and dive into the weird and wonderful world of Wednesday Addams. Seeing life through her lens will help you feel stronger, more capable and more authentically you than ever before.

Seven rules to live by

You'll find everything you need to embrace your dark side and thrive in this book. But if you're after a quick guide to get you started, look no further than these seven golden rules to live by. Try one out each day of the week and by the time your next Wednesday comes around, you'll be living your life just for you.

1. Set your boundaries. Check them again.

2. Step away from people who aren't rooting for you – and surround yourself with people who are.

3. Indulge your passions, and feel zero shame about it.

4. Go right ahead and do that thing you want to do.

5. Invite your TRUE personality to step out of the shadows.

6. Feel the fear, and do it anyway.

7. Accept that you can't please all of the people, all of the time. Welcome to your villain era!

Family

Like a lot of people, Wednesday sometimes finds her family excruciating. And if we're honest, her folks are pretty out there. While they might be unconventional (not many parents would let their children roam freely in a cemetery, build an electric chair or encourage an interest in taxidermy), Morticia and Gomez support Wednesday's creativity and celebrate both their children fiercely. They have never been bound by the expectations of 'polite' society. They play golf from the rooftops, chop the heads off roses, and have created a striking yet spooky home in which their family can grow and experiment without persecution.

For one thing, Wednesday's parents are still madly in love with each other and are the very best of friends, even after years of marriage. They enjoy a deeply passionate partnership and they're outwardly very affectionate with each other. And while public displays of affection aren't Wednesday's thing, even she knows you have to admire that kind of happy longevity in a relationship.

The Addams family children have a lot more freedom than most of their peers, and they're given plenty of space to explore all their own passions and hobbies, something that helps them develop resilience and trust in their own abilities from a young age.

Their wider family members and friends, like Cousin Itt, Lurch and Uncle Fester, are all pretty unusual, too. But everyone in the Addams family accepts and loves them for what makes them different. So while they're all far from perfect, there's a lot of love in the Addams family, and Wednesday has grown up in the thick of it.

Wednesday's relationship with her mother

Morticia is sometimes tricky. But despite the emotional tussle between them, their bond is strong, and whether it's music, reading or carnivorous plants, they often find they have common ground. It's the same for Wednesday and her younger brother, Pugsley. Because they've grown up playing together, they share a lot of the same passions, and even though she finds him annoying sometimes, Wednesday won't let anyone harm him.

Being the oldest child often comes with a burden of responsibility, however strange your family's definition of responsibility might be. Being that child in such an unusual family isn't always easy for Wednesday to navigate. Still, it turns out that all of these feelings and frustrations are pretty normal for everyone. It's part of the process of growing and finding your feet. For all their faults and differences, underneath it all, Wednesday's love for her family is boundless. They taught her to be herself and find strength in being different from the crowd. They gave her a whole bunch of life skills that most people don't ever acquire. They're always rooting for her, and woe betide anyone who tries to hurt them. They might be monsters, but they're her monsters. There is a lot that we can learn from the Addams' family values.

Mine your ancestry for answers

One of Wednesday's great idols is her Great Aunt Calpurnia, who was known for dancing naked in the streets and enchanting church ministers, and was eventually burned at the stake as a witch. What a woman! It may not be a coincidence, then, that when it comes to injustices made by those in power against anyone vulnerable or in the minority, Wednesday always feels empowered to stand up for what is right.

Engaging with the experiences of your ancestors can be a wonderful way to explore your own identity and connect with a deeper part of yourself. But it can also be challenging, so take care of yourself in this process. Remember that the past is never a blueprint for your present, but it can shine a light on your path and help you understand the people around you. Take the time to speak to older generations or to brush up on your family history – you never know what you might find out.

Keep your siblings
(or someone like them) close

Pugsley, Wednesday's younger brother, can be a strange boy. It would be easy for Wednesday to dismiss Pugsley in favour of more sophisticated folk, but even though she does like to torture him from time to time, Wednesday knows Pugsley needs her to look out for him and she knows she kind of needs him, too. No one else quite understands what it's like to grow up in her family. And no one else but Pugsley shares her passion for spiders and dynamite and slicing the heads off dolls. Even though he's annoying at times, Wednesday sees Pugsley as a true ally, and the bond they share is something she can always rely on.

You might not always appreciate the quirks of your siblings (road-sign kleptomania or a worrying obsession with explosives can be particularly hazardous) but strong relationships with your siblings can come in handy when you need someone around you who understands you. If you don't have any siblings, or things are not straightforward for you on that front, you can often find the same kind of allyship in a good friend. Look out for those friendships that feel unconditional and hold them close.

Find your chosen family

Some of us don't have a tight-knit family unit around us. And some of us need to set some pretty firm boundaries with the families we are born into. Everyone is different and having a different setup doesn't make us any more or less worthy of the love and support we all need. It's good to remember that you don't always have to be related to someone to feel like they're family. We all have special and important people in our lives who mean just as much to us – and sometimes more – as our birth families. Look to the other people around you – your coaches, employers and friends – for the helping hand you need, especially when you don't feel able to go to your biological family. Extended family members like grandparents, aunts and uncles can sometimes be very handy. Wednesday's Uncle Fester proves to be an extremely valuable asset time and time again, and so does her much-loved appendage, Thing.

These kinds of people often have a different perspective on life, and different skills, and they can offer support and guidance in new ways. Look to your extended or chosen family to make sure you feel supported and have loving guidance in everything you do.

'No one torments my family but me.'

*'Sic gorgiamus allos
subjectatos nunc'*

We gladly feast on those
who would subdue us

THE FAMILY MOTTO

'All families are strange.'

TIM BURTON

Friends

From the outside it can sometimes seem like Wednesday doesn't really need or want any friends. With her unflinching stare, her dark, foreboding get-up and that general air of suppressed fury, it would be easy to conclude that Wednesday Addams simply wants to be alone. But what Wednesday lacks in superficial positivity and pointless niceties, she more than makes up for with her fierce sense of loyalty and justice — two things that, as it turns out, make her pretty much the best friend anyone could ask for.

Wednesday and her brother were cage-schooled by Lurch when they were young, so it's only later in life that Wednesday begins to form significant bonds with people her own age outside of her family. And although she's not the life of the party (unless there's dancing), and despite her need for solitude, Wednesday emerges as a savage protector of her pals, especially of those who are vulnerable, struggling or rejected by the status quo.

Wednesday can be quite rigid and assertive — she definitely isn't concerned with making people like her — but she is always open to learning new things from others, and often makes friends with the most unexpected people, especially those who are very different to her. So while she is always down for a little pain and torture, that never includes hurting people who can't protect themselves.

She's also not keen on fitting in with the 'it' crowd, no matter how unusual that crowd may be. Maybe it's because she was born into such an unusual family, or maybe it's because she knows the 'it' crowd isn't really it at all, and they are all, in fact, shapeshifters pretending to be people they're not. Either way, she learned early on that she can survive and thrive without needing validation from anyone else or shrinking herself to fit the needs of others. In a world where her peers are all about allegiance to a certain group or fashion, Wednesday has simply never been bothered about joining a gang or aligning herself with anyone else's values. Authenticity like Wednesday's usually comes at a cost — she knows when to set a boundary and people don't always know how to handle it. But she sleeps soundly at night, knowing that she's been authentically herself, all day long.

Be real

Wednesday never compromises her true self in order to make herself popular. While it might make fitting in more difficult at first, in the long run, it means she knows people really like her and care about her for who she is. Sometimes it's hard to be true to yourself if you're not quite sure who that is. It's OK to explore different options and to experiment with different versions of you. No one gets to decide who you are but you. Make time to get to know yourself, what you need, and how you can be the best version of yourself. Always stay true to your needs, even if that means people don't always understand.

Celebrate the differences

Wednesday knows there is strength and power in enjoying each other's differences. She isn't only kind of different herself, she is drawn to people who are quite different from her. Try not to worry about fitting in with the crowd; instead, don't be afraid to get deep. Talk about the things that make you different and find out more about what makes the people you meet different, too. What do they like? What excites them? You might be surprised by the answer.

Alone doesn't equal lonely

Wednesday isn't into being part of big friendship groups or having really intense friendships. She knows that keeping up too many connections can be emotionally draining, and she knows when she needs to take time for her. She's also not afraid to stay away from friendships that don't serve her. But even with the friends she really loves and values, Wednesday often needs her own space. If you're an introvert like Wednesday, and even if you're not, it's important to find time for a little peace and quiet, just for you. Set some clear boundaries with your friends about when you need time out and communicate your needs clearly so that they know what to expect. Then enjoy recharging your batteries in a way that is nourishing and healthful for you.

'Wednesday, look at all of the other children, their freckles, their bright little eyes, their eager, friendly smiles. Help them.'

MORTICIA

'She's the perfect student – a gifted polyglot, cellist, novelist and fencer . . . but still, she finds herself an outcast.'

'Today's young people deserve to have their own version of Wednesday.'

CHRISTINA RICCI

Home

Much like her family, Wednesday's family home is not your regular run-of-the-mill mansion. To a lot of people, it probably looks a bit spooky and old-fashioned. Some rumours suggest it was once an asylum, others say it was condemned. But let's face it, the Addams aren't really into picket fences and roses around the door. They'd rather bury the Joneses than keep up with them. And despite its haunted-looking exterior, the big old house on Cemetery Lane was a fun place for a girl to grow up.

All those long corridors and dusty rooms full of books and art meant Wednesday learned early on how to make her own fun, usually torturing Pugsley or playing with sharp objects. Her parents were always busy doing something, so she learned to explore and came to value books and being able to curl up in a quiet corner with her favourite children's book, *Frankenstein*. Living by candlelight all those years means she's not afraid of the dark, in fact, it's where she feels safest — plus she's the queen of an atmospheric lighting scheme. Knocking around in a big house like that also helped Wednesday to appreciate her own space and how, even if the rest of the house is covered in cobwebs, it doesn't take much to make a space your own.

Personal space is important to Wednesday and she has been known, when sharing a dorm, to create a visible boundary — not to be hostile but to make sure everyone knows where her space is.

For Wednesday, her room is an expression of who she is, just like her clothes, and she embraces the same dark colours and vintage vibe in her interiors as she does in her clothes. But although she likes her old-fashioned furniture and shuns all the sleek and shiny newness of modern life, she's also not one for too much clutter. Perhaps because the rest of the house she grew up in was so busy and full of interesting things (who else had a bear-skin rug that growled at the guests?) or perhaps because she feels calmer when everything around her is simple, Wednesday keeps a clear desk and she always makes her bed. Starting the day with this easy accomplishment helps her feel like she's winning from the minute she wakes up. Which, of course, she is.

Dial up your personality to the max

Wednesday loves black and uses the warmth in dark colours to feel safe and cosy in her own space and to reflect her personality. Think about the colours that make you feel safe or at home – how can you use them in your space? If painting your whole room isn't an option, think about bringing in your favourite colours or patterns with textiles like cushions and rugs. Even just painting the frame on a picture or mirror can change how a room feels and better reflect your personality.

Make space for you

It's super important for Wednesday to make her space her own. We all need a space that's our own, no matter how small. If you don't have a room for yourself or can't change what's already there, try curating a smaller space within a room where you can just be and enjoy feeling authentically you. This could be a desk where you sit to read, or a mantlepiece full of your favourite pieces, even just a windowsill with your favourite plants on. It doesn't need to be big, expensive and impressive, it's about making a space that's all yours. Look after this space, keep it clean and make it somewhere you can go to and feel relaxed and harmonious.

Look to the past

You don't always need to go out and get new stuff to make over a room. A piece or two of old furniture or an old print for your wall can really ground a space and give it a sense of character. Plus, it's a great way to recycle and save money for your other hobbies. If you are working to a budget, try scouring your local vintage or secondhand shops, you never know what you might find. If you don't have a very big budget, what can you dig out from your own personal history and upcycle, to add character to your room?

'There's nothing more romantic than a dark chill attic in a thunderstorm.'

MORTICIA

'Every room needs a touch of black, just as it needs one antique piece.'

'A woman must have money and a room of her own if she is to write fiction.'

Virginia Woolf

Style

Like any global style icon, Wednesday knows the power of owning her look. She isn't fussed by the fleeting fripperies of fashion, Wednesday's vibe is defined by her commitment to the dark side: black is the new black, sometimes with a statement red lipstick. But she's also got one foot in the past, with her A-line dresses and neat long plaits serving a side dish of vintage, because only someone as dead cool as Wednesday knows that being timeless is to die for.

Wednesday picked up a lot of her style cues from her mother Morticia. She doesn't dress exactly like her — Morticia is a masterclass in old-school gothic glamour, wearing her trademark jet-black, bias-cut dress and poker-straight raven hair at all times. But she is descended from witches — Morticia's family tree goes back to Salem — and like her ancestors, Wednesday has inherited a love of dark and striking attire. The pretty pinks and pastels worn by some girls in order to look more feminine are not of interest to Wednesday. She would never conform to someone else's idea of what it is to be a girl, or a boy — or indeed anyone other than herself.

There's also a highly practical element to Wednesday's look — dark colours don't show the dirt so much and require far less washing and general maintenance than pale or colourful clothes. This is good news for Wednesday, who not only shares her mother's disinterest in laundry and other forms of domestic slavery, but tends to get dirty jousting and fencing, digging up graves and generally being hands-on in everything she does. Dark colours are also better for blending into the background, and occasionally the night — two of the places where Wednesday feels most comfortable.

But having a style all of her own doesn't mean she is predictable or dull. Wednesday is the master of playful riffs on regular wardrobe staples. Check out those oversize power collars, sheesh! And while most of her peers seem to go for more casual looks, Wednesday usually likes to fix up sharp. Why? Because Wednesday Addams always mean business.

Hair is key

Wednesday's plaits might look cute, but Wednesday couldn't be further from cute, and there is method to those butter-wouldn't-melt braids. Not only are they striking and easy to do yourself, you can also hide all sorts of useful items inside them. Braids also keep your hair out of the way when you're busy, be it vivisecting bodies or writing your novel. If braids aren't your thing, try a top-knot, a high ponytail or even a buzz cut. Find the statement style that speaks to you. And when you fancy a switch-up, a blunt, heavy fringe makes a big statement and is great for keeping your emotions hidden from view.

Big collars are the bomb

Nothing says you mean business more than a crisp white shirt with huge pointy collars, right? Shirt collars somehow suggest efficiency and extraordinary intellect. They also bring an androgynous vibe to your outfit that keeps you well out of anyone's unhelpful gendered pigeonholes. Add some cuffs for full effect. Wear with everything and watch as the world bows down. If you don't think collars are for you, experiment with your own statement motif or accessories – anything from a big belt to a trademark oversize hairbow could work – and find the thing that makes you feel good.

Embrace the darkness

In a world full of colour, Wednesday knows that black makes her stand out. You don't have to go full-monochrome, but there is a lot of freedom to be had in finding your own colour or palette of colours and sticking with it. The colours you gravitate towards and choose to wear can speak volumes about who you are and, if you love them as much as Wednesday loves black, will make you feel more confident and happy about the way you look. Different colours can also have an amazing effect on your own colouring and bring out aspects and features you didn't know could pop so hard! Plus, sticking to a colour palette takes a lot of stress out of shopping. Focus on a few key pieces and styles to try out different colours and see what works for you!

'The little black dress is a
classic, Mother.'

'Refusing to conform to patriarchal and social norms, Wednesday is awkward, wherein lies much of her appeal.'

'Wednesday changed my taste a lot. I have a hard time getting her off of me, at least clothing-wise.'

JENNA ORTEGA

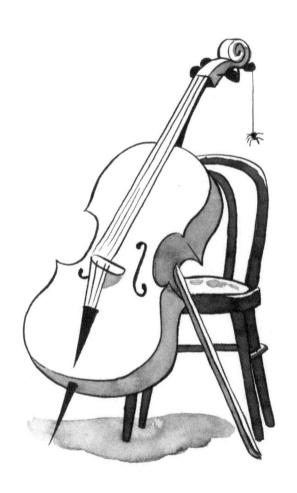

Music

usic is extremely important to Wednesday, and she uses it in so many different and positive ways.

You could say she had a musical upbringing: her mother Morticia plays the Japanese shamisen, an instrument that is kind of like a banjo with a long neck and three strings, and the violin. So it's not surprising that Wednesday eventually picked up an instrument herself. Wednesday has been known to be a brilliant cellist, and she regularly makes time to play — not only classical music but also modern songs with a twist from the timeless sound of her instrument. Playing an instrument can give you peace when everything around you is feeling overwhelming, not only because of the music but because it's also such a physical experience, involving the whole body and using all your motor skills — you really have to focus. But of course the deep and mournful sound of a string instrument in particular appeals to Wednesday, especially when she needs time to think and process her feelings away from other people.

Wednesday doesn't only play her own music, she enjoys listening to it as well. She likes to play deeply moving and emotive music like the Mexican folk songs of La Llorona (the weeping woman) while she is writing, perhaps because they remind her of her father.

She knows how to move, too. As a little girl, Wednesday did ballet in a black leotard and tutu and often did recitals for her doting parents. She also liked contemporary dance and taught Lurch to do all the latest dances, including the Droop. Dance was in the family: as well as Mexican heritage, Wednesday has Cossack ancestors and she grew up watching all the men in the Addams family dance the Mamushka — a dance of brotherly love that they perform when celebrating. All of this experience has given Wednesday the confidence to really throw some unusual shapes. Her style of dancing as though no one is watching is truly unique, but also so infectious that it gets everyone up on the dance floor.

Step out of your comfort zone

Wednesday doesn't only appreciate classical music. From the sweeping classical notes to the rock and roll of The Cramps, she isn't afraid to mix up her genres and experiment with the status quo. There's so much music out there, you don't need to stick to one sound or genre. Make time to listen to songs you might not normally choose and see what you think – it could be the beginning of a new obsession!

Look to your heritage

It's easy to dismiss the old music that your folks listen to as being out of touch or having nothing to say. And it's true, new sounds can feel so exciting and zeitgeisty. But take the time to read up on musical movements of the past and listen to some of the songs that you think are too old for your tastes. There are some epic stories and legendary personalities behind the music of the past, whether it's rock and roll feuds or the struggles that inspired some of the great protest songs. See what you can discover simply by listening to music; it will broaden your knowledge and horizons immeasurably.

Share music with others

Wednesday might reach for the cello when she needs some time for herself, but growing up with all those Addams' family dances and celebrations, she also knows the value of sharing music with your friends and family. With today's personalised playlists and headphones, it's all too easy to see listening to music as an escape and something you do by yourself. Don't forget to share the joy, though – make listening to music something you enjoy with your friends and family.

'My holiday playlist is titled Pugsley's Greatest Screams.'

'Ah, sweet music!'

'Slay Wednesday! You're welcome at Haus of Gaga anytime . . . and bring Thing with you.'

LADY GAGA

Work

Wednesday doesn't technically have a job yet, but that doesn't stop her from applying her many skills to some very important projects. In fact, she's often the one showing others how to do their jobs. She has confidence beyond her years and shows unusual commitment to every project she gets involved in.

But although she is very industrious, let's face it, Wednesday isn't ever going to work for someone else. When she sees an opportunity to do something, she tends to go for it, whether or not it's against the rules or the law. That can sometimes get her into trouble. But you know what? She may not always toe the line, but all that chutzpah is a great quality to have around the place, and her enthusiasm for her latest experiment or investigation always rubs off on those around her.

Because she hasn't always had a lot of friends, Wednesday learned early on the art of occupying herself and making the most of her resources. So she's not afraid of solitude; it gives her space to think, which means she's usually happier working alone. It also means she's developed a lot of self-discipline and doesn't ever need an excuse to sneak away from a party to study or investigate her latest mystery.

Sometimes these qualities can work against her; she can find it hard to work as part of a team or to share her thoughts and feelings with colleagues and peers. But the upside is, she's not someone who wastes time on point-less activities — and this is especially true now with the distractions of the online world and social media. Instead, Wednesday throws her full self into everything she does with a singular approach and the kind of focus most of us can only dream about. The result? The girl gets things done.

Be a self-starter

Have you ever had a great idea but
never done anything about it
because you thought you shouldn't,
or couldn't? That is so Tuesday.
Wednesday would not sit around
waiting for other people to tell her
what she can do, and nor should
you. If you have a great idea or see
an opportunity to do something
good, grab it by both horns!

Develop your focus

Wednesday is someone who always sees things through, even if it lands her in hot water sometimes. Her capacity for focus and perseverance is boundless. If you struggle to stay focused on things at work, don't just write yourself off as someone with a short attention span and skip gaily onto the next thing. Persevere! Try training your focus muscle. Phones can be especially distracting and have you jumping from image to image like Thing on hot coals. Give yourself plenty of time away from your phone (at bedtime especially) and try to nourish your mind with things that require your concentration, in a way you enjoy. We're talking music, crafts like sewing and painting, maybe learning a language or an instrument.

Have a plan

Wednesday has a clear vision of who and where she wants to be – or doesn't want to be. If something doesn't fit into her plan then she tends not to engage with it. You don't have to stick rigidly to your own plan, but having a vision about where you're going in life and what you want to achieve is a great way to help you navigate your career. It doesn't need to be anything sophisticated, you can just write it down, or if you are a visual person, try making a mood board. Cut out pictures of the people and places that inspire you and use it to help you stay on track.

'Do something interesting with your time and don't worry about what people think of you. Because there is no normal.'

'I know I'm stubborn,
single-minded and obsessive.
But those are all traits of
great writers . . . And
serial killers.'

'Ah now I understand. This is a children's prison.'

Creativity

For Wednesday, creativity is life. Whether it's writing her novel or recreating dramatic scenes and sword-fights, she is never happier than when she's immersed fully in her creative process.

Perhaps unsurprisingly, she grew up in a family where being creative was not only encouraged but a necessary part of family life. As well as a passionate shamisen player, Morticia is an innovative cook who always wows the family with her new and unusual creations — eye of newt, anyone? She's also an original painter and devoted gardener, and the children knew from a young age that their mother was not to be disturbed while she was engaged in her passions — something that instilled a respect for the creative process in the young Wednesday. Without the distractions of modern technology and few friends to play with other than Pugsley, Wednesday was encouraged to be creative and come up with her own games and activities. And when she wasn't creating things for herself, she was inspired by the art and books and music that surrounded her in the family home.

Being naturally inclined to introversion gives Wednesday plenty of time to think, reflect and have ideas. It also means she's often happier expressing her feelings in ways other than talking out loud — perhaps that's why she loves to write and play music. But being creative isn't only about expressing herself. The time she spends immersed in her creative zone is a kind of safe space for her where she can combine physical and mental activities and enter a state of true flow. Sometimes this can make her seem a bit cut off from everyone else, but those who know her understand that she is taking it all in and making sense of the world through her creative output.

Prioritise your practice

Wednesday learned from her mother that making time for creativity is not a luxury but a necessity for her own wellbeing and peace of mind. Make sure you put time in your schedule for your creative practice and never apologise or make excuses for doing so! Getting better at anything requires practice, and creativity is no exception, so back yourself, make time for your innovations and enjoy the sense of growth and accomplishment that comes as you progress on your creative journey.

Boost your creativity

If you're feeling blocked or uninspired,
make like Wednesday and get outside of
your head for a boost. Try doing
something to get your body
moving. Focusing on doing something
physical, be it yoga or kickboxing, let the
creative part of your brain work away
unhindered in the background for a while,
and you'll often find that big ideas come
naturally after some kind of physical
exercise. Exercise is also a great way to
boost your mood and keep you going if
you're feeling low. It's a win-win!

Dig where you stand

Have you ever felt like you really want to write something but don't know what to write about? Are you into pottery but don't want to make another boring generic vase? Digging where you stand means taking inspiration from the people, places and things around you that are unique to you. It's easy to imagine that people won't be interested in your themes and stories, but these are the things that make you special and interesting. They are also often the things that others can relate to. By sharing your personal experiences and what you see and hear around you, you can challenge preconceptions or reach out to other people who might be feeling the same way. Next time you're feeling stuck, look at what's in front of you or ask yourself how you are feeling right now, and start with that. You never know where it might take you.

'Wednesday, play with your food.'

MORTICIA

'Great thinkers need obstacles
to function.'

'Wednesday has endured as a character because she's not afraid to be bold.'

Love

Wednesday's parents, Gomez and Morticia, are passionately in love with each other and they like to make very public displays of affection — something Wednesday finds hard to stomach at times. Nobody wants to see their parents continually locked in a tight embrace.

Still, you might imagine that growing up with all of that mutual admiration would have rubbed off on Wednesday just a little bit. But you'd be wrong. Wednesday rarely shows signs of wanting that kind of overt physical affection, or indeed of needing anyone at all.

But that doesn't mean she's not interested in connecting with others. Most human beings want connection and companionship, and Wednesday is no different. It's just that she communicates and receives love in different ways.

Instead of big gestures, gifts and emotional language or expression, Wednesday shows her love to people — whoever they are — with deeds instead of words, and by simply spending time with them. Maybe this is a result of growing up without a smartphone, or maybe it's a response to her parents, or maybe it's just who she is. Whatever the reason, the important thing for Wednesday is that she shows people how much she cares about them in a way that feels comfortable and true for her.

Gender roles or any other heteronormative constructs are unimportant to Wednesday. Sure, she's made some mistakes when it comes to the game of love, but who hasn't? Wednesday knows that love — whether it's romantic or platonic — is a journey and that sometimes it's OK to trip up, take wrong turns and double back if you need to.

And while she might find her parents' mutual appreciation a bit much at times, what she did take from their example is the right not to feel guilty about companionship and seeking her pleasure as a young woman, in a sometimes still surprisingly puritanical world.

Most importantly, Wednesday won't shrink herself in order to get or maintain a relationship — why would you pretend to be someone you're not just so you can have a relationship? For Wednesday, the most important relationship she has is with herself, and she knows that as long as that is running smoothly, everything else will, too.

Love yourself

Wednesday prioritises her self-care, celebrates what makes her unique and she never shrinks herself to fit into anyone else's idea of how she should be. This doesn't mean she's being selfish, it means that she recognises the importance of self-preservation and lives life on her terms. Think about how you treat the people you love and ask yourself if you treat yourself in the same way. Do you treat yourself well and with kindness? How we treat ourselves often becomes what we will tolerate from others, so we need to make sure we are setting that bar high. We all deserve love and respect, and that starts from within.

Learn your love language

Everyone connects and communicates affection with their loved ones in different ways. Wednesday expresses her feelings by consistently showing up for the people she cares about, and by giving them her time and attention. How do you communicate your feelings, and how do you want to receive love from others? Thinking about this and identifying your (and your partners') love languages can help you and everyone in your relationships feel closer. Communicate your needs and boundaries clearly and listen to what your partners need, too, for a deeper understanding and a more equal relationship.

Be a boundary boss

Setting boundaries about how you want to be loved and cared for isn't about putting up walls to keep people out, it's about inviting the right people in, and those boundaries go both ways. Wednesday is adept at staying true to herself and not allowing others to compromise her in exchange for their company or affection. Is there someone in your life who you feel takes more than they give? Or someone who seems to drain you of your energy? It could be time to politely put in place some boundaries and turn your attention to the people and relationships that serve you best – even if it means making other people uncomfortable or being the villain in someone else's story. Any partner should enrich your life just as you enrich theirs, not become a drain on it. If you consistently find your boundaries aren't being respected and you can't find common ground, it might be time to step away.

Joel: 'But what if you met just the right man, who worshipped and adored you, who'd do anything you say, who'd be your devoted slave? Then what would you do?'

Wednesday: 'I'd pity him.'

Lurch: 'I like being miserable.'

Wednesday: 'You might find a nice girl to be miserable with.'

'She's unapologetic, fearless, smart, weird — it's very rare to see a female teen character who's that sure of herself.'

JENNA ORTEGA

List Seven Things That Bring You Joy

1.

2.

3.

4.

5.

6.

7.

List Seven Things You Want to Learn

1.

2.

3.

4.

5.

6.

7.

List Seven Things You Value in Relationships

1.

2.

3.

4.

5.

6.

7.

List Seven Ways You Communicate Love

1.

2.

3.

4.

5.

6.

7.

Acknowledgements

The Addams Family is a fictional family created by American cartoonist Charles Addams. Wednesday Addams and her family originally appeared in a series of 150 single-panel comics, some of which were originally published in *The New Yorker* between 1938 and their creator's death in 1988. The Addams Family was subsequently popularised in various film and TV adaptations.

p27 from *The Addams Family* animated movie, 2019 (Conrad Vernon, Greg Tiernan; Bron Creative, Metro-Goldwyn-Mayer, The Jackal Group, Cinesite Studios, Nitrogen Studios), p28 from *The Addams Family* feature film, 1991 (Barry Sonnenfeld; Paramount Pictures, Scott Rudin Productions), p29 from 'Behind the Scenes' Tim Burton on Netflix's *Wednesday*, October 2022, p39 from *The Addams Family Values*, 1993 (Barry Sonnenfeld; Scott Rudin Productions), p40 from *The Guardian*, 'How Netflix's Wednesday Became a Pop Culture Phenomenon', 14 December, 2022, p41 from *The Independent*, 'Christina Ricci Shares Her Thoughts on Jenna Ortega's Wednesday', 26 December, 2022, p51 from *The Addams Family* television series, 1964 (Filmways Television), p52 from Jan Showers, Essentialhome.eu. May, 2017, p53 from *A Room of One's Own*, by Virginia Woolf, 1929, p63 from *The Addams Family 2* animated movie, 2021 (Conrad Vernon, Greg Tiernan, Laura Brousseau; Bron Creative, Metro-Goldwyn-Mayer, Cinesite Studios, Nitrogen Studios, The Jackal Group, Glickmania), p64 from *The Guardian*, 'Her Dark Materials', 14 December, 2022, p65 from *Teen Vogue*, 'Jenna Ortega Opened Up About How Much Wednesday Influenced Her Own Style', 10 March, 2023, p75 from Wednesday Addams on Twitter, 22 November, 2022, p76 from *The Addams Family*, Series 1 Episode 7, animated series, 1992 (Robert Alvarez, Don Lusk, Carl Urbano; H-B Production Co.), p77 from Lady Gaga on Twitter, 1 December, 2022, p87 from *The Independent*, 'Why Does Wednesday Addams Continue to Matter?', 29 November, 2022, p88 from *Wednesday*, Netflix, 2022 (Tim Burton, James Marshall, Gandja Monteiro; MGM Television, Millar Gough Ink, Tim Burton *Productions*, Toluca Pictures), p89 from *The Addams Family* animated movie, 2019 (Conrad Vernon, Greg Tiernan; Bron Creative, Metro-Goldwyn-Mayer, The Jackal Group, Cinesite Studios, Nitrogen Studios), p99 from *The Addams Family* feature film, 1991 (Barry Sonnenfeld; Paramount Pictures, Scott Rudin Productions), p100 from *The Addams Family 2* animated movie, 2021 (Conrad Vernon, Greg Tiernan, Laura Brousseau; Bron Creative, Metro-Goldwyn-Mayer, Cinesite Studios, Nitrogen Studios, The Jackal Group, Glickmania), p101 from *The New York Times*, 'Dance Like You're Wednesday Addams', 19 January, 2023, pp111–12 from *The Addams Family Values*, 1993 (Barry Sonnenfeld; Scott Rudin Productions), pp113–14 from *The Addams Family* television series, 1964 (Filmways Television), p115 from *The New York Times*, 'Jenna Ortega Knows What Wednesday Addams Wants', 23 November, 2022.

4

Published in 2023 by Pop Press an imprint of Ebury Publishing, 20 Vauxhall Bridge Road, London SW1V 2SA

Pop Press is part of the Penguin Random House group of companies whose addresses can be found at global.penguinrandomhouse.com

Text © Pop Press 2023

Text: Sarah Thompson
Illustrations: Ollie Mann
Text Design: Ed Pickford

www.penguin.co.uk

A CIP catalogue record for this book is available from the British Library

ISBN 9781529915471

Typeset in 13/16pt Marco Polo by Jouve (UK), Milton Keynes
Printed and bound in Great Britain by Clays Ltd, Elcograf S.p.A.

The authorised representative in the EEA is Penguin Random House Ireland, Morrison Chambers, 32 Nassau Street, Dublin D02 YH68

Penguin Random House is committed to a sustainable future for our business, our readers and our planet. This book is made from Forest Stewardship Council® certified paper.